Machines to the Rescue

Helicopters

by Bizzy Harris

Bullfrog Books

Ideas for Parents and Teachers

Bullfrog Books let children practice reading informational text at the earliest reading levels. Repetition, familiar words, and photo labels support early readers.

Before Reading

- Discuss the cover photo. What does it tell them?
- Look at the picture glossary together. Read and discuss the words.

Read the Book

- "Walk" through the book and look at the photos. Let the child ask questions. Point out the photo labels.
- Read the book to the child, or have him or her read independently.

After Reading

- Prompt the child to think more. Ask: Have you ever heard or seen a helicopter? Would you like to?

Bullfrog Books are published by Jump!
5357 Penn Avenue South
Minneapolis, MN 55419
www.jumplibrary.com

Library of Congress Cataloging-in-Publication Data

Names: Harris, Bizzy, author.
Title: Helicopters / by Bizzy Harris.
Description: Minneapolis, MN: Jump!, Inc., [2022]
Series: Machines to the rescue | Includes index.
Audience: Ages 5–8 | Audience: Grades K–1
Identifiers: LCCN 2020041883 (print)
LCCN 2020041884 (ebook)
ISBN 9781645279105 (hardcover)
ISBN 9781645279112 (paperback)
ISBN 9781645279129 (ebook)
Subjects: LCSH: Helicopters—Juvenile literature.
Helicopters in search and rescue operations
Juvenile literature.
Classification: LCC TL716.2 .H367 2022 (print)
LCC TL716.2 (ebook) | DDC 629.133/352—dc23
LC record available at https://lccn.loc.gov/2020041883
LC ebook record available at https://lccn.loc.gov/2020041884

Editor: Jenna Gleisner
Designer: Molly Ballanger

Photo Credits: Iakov Filimonov/Shutterstock, cover; 1001Love/iStock, 1; suriyasilsaksom/iStock, 3; ABBYDOG/Shutterstock, 4; Balefire9/Dreamstime, 5 (background); Krakenimages.com/Shutterstock, 5 (foreground); Darren Baker/Dreamstime, 6–7, 23br; rbkomar/Shutterstock, 8; Artistic Ahry/Shutterstock, 9; millsrymer/iStock, 10–11; U.S. Coast Guard, 12–13, 14–15, 18–19, 23tr, 23tm, 23bl; VCNW/Getty, 16–17, 23tl;
gubernat/Shutterstock, 19, 23bm; Drew Horne/ Shutterstock, 20–21; Supertrooper/Shutterstock, 22; Brian Finestone/Shutterstock, 24.

Printed in India.

Table of Contents

Fly Up High

Helicopters fly.
We call them choppers.

They are loud.
Whop! Whop!

They fly up.

They fly down.

They even fly side to side!

They fly over water.

They fly over peaks. Cool!

This one fights fires.
How?
It dumps water.

water

This crew is in a hurry.

Why?

A person needs help!

A pilot flies.
She sits in the cockpit.

cockpit

The chopper takes off.
Its blades spin.

Its tail has blades, too.
They help steer.

The chopper hovers.
The crew looks.
They see the man.
They rescue him!

skid

The chopper lands on skids.

It lands on a roof.

Wow!

Parts of a Helicopter

Take a look at the parts of a helicopter!

Picture Glossary

blades
The long, flat parts of a rotor that spin to lift a helicopter.

cockpit
The area in a plane, boat, or helicopter where a pilot sits.

crew
The group of people who operate a vehicle.

hovers
Remains in one place in the air.

rescue
To save from danger.

steer
To make a vehicle move in a particular direction.

Index

To Learn More

Finding more information is as easy as 1, 2, 3.

1. Go to www.factsurfer.com
2. Enter "helicopters" into the search box.
3. Choose your book to see a list of websites.